KU-782-418

FOCUS ON

THE HUMAN BODY

STEVE PARKER

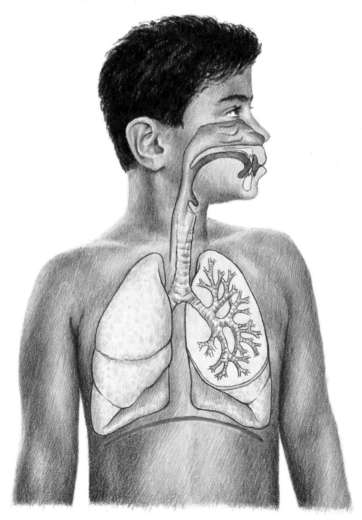

Aladdin/Watts
London • Sydney

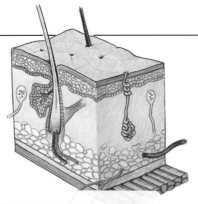

ABERDEENSHIRE LIBRARY AND INFORMATION SERVICE	
1642529	
CAW	293392
J612	£11.99
JU	KINP

This edition published 2003
© Aladdin Books Ltd 2003
All rights reserved

Designed and produced by
Aladdin Books Ltd
28 Percy Street
London W1T 2BZ

First published in
Great Britain in 1993 by
Watts Books
96 Leonard Street
London EC2A 4XD

ISBN 0 7496 5076 1

A CIP catalogue record for this book is available from the British Library.

Printed in UAE

Design	David West Children's Book Design
Designer	Flick Killerby
Series Director	Bibby Whittaker
Editor	Jen Green
Picture research	Emma Krikler
Illustrators	David Burroughs Biz Hull

The author, Steve Parker, is a writer and editor in the life sciences, health and medicine, who has written many books for children on science and nature.

The consultant, Dr Sue Green, received her MBChB in 1978 and has been a general practitioner for many years.

INTRODUCTION

Each of us possesses one of the most complex devices in the universe – a human body. Yet few of us have read the owner's manual. This book provides a biological background to the body, its structures and systems. It includes information about human history and different ways of life around the world. It describes how the human body has featured in many works of literature, and has formed the basis for words and phrases in many languages. It shows that the body has also been a springboard for the progress of science through the ages, and records some of the milestones in that process. The key below shows how these subjects are divided up throughout the book.

Geography
The symbol of the planet Earth indicates where geographical facts and activities are examined in this book. These sections include a discussion of how human bodies and customs vary in different parts of the globe.

Language and literature
An open book is the sign for activities and information about language and literature. The prowess of the human body is the subject of tales and legends in many cultures. Some of these stories are examined in these sections.

Science and maths
The microscope symbol shows where information or activities about science or maths subjects are included. These sections include a look at the nutritional value of different kinds of foods.

History
The sign of the scroll and hourglass indicates where historical information is given. These sections examine how understanding of the human body has changed over the centuries. They focus on key scientists and physicians.

Social history
The symbol of the family indicates where information about social history is given. These sections provide an insight into ideas about the body and medical beliefs that exist in different cultures.

Art, craft and music
The symbol showing a sheet of music and art tools signals where activities and information about art, craft and music are given. The human body has inspired artists, sculptors and musicians all over the world.

CONTENTS

STRUCTURE AND SYSTEMS

The human body, and especially the brain that controls it, are extremely complicated and truly amazing. Even so, scientists now understand much of the body's structure, or anatomy, and how the body works. Like all living things, the body is made up of tiny units called cells. There are many different types of cells in the body, doing different jobs. Cells combine with others of the same type to form tissues. Various tissues combine to form the body's main parts, the organs, and the organs combine to make working systems.

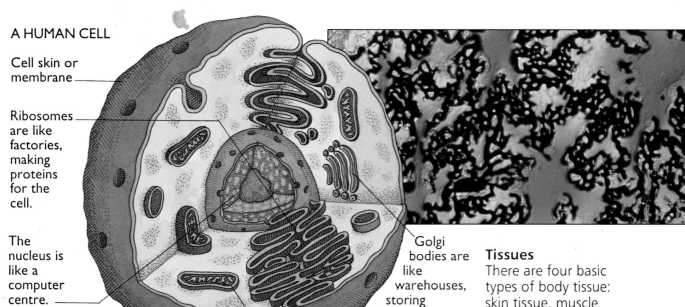

A HUMAN CELL

Cell skin or membrane

Ribosomes are like factories, making proteins for the cell.

The nucleus is like a computer centre.

Golgi bodies are like warehouses, storing proteins.

Mitochondria are like power stations, supplying energy for life.

Inside a cell
A cell contains even smaller parts known as organelles, such as ribosomes, above. Each is like a mini-organ, with a special job to do. The nucleus is the cell's control centre and contains the genetic material, DNA (see page 29).

Tissues
There are four basic types of body tissue: skin tissue, muscle tissue, nerve tissue, and connective tissue (above), which includes bone, cartilage and fat.

Body organisation
The basic building-blocks of the human body, and of all other living things, are cells. These microscopic objects are the smallest units capable of the vast range of chemical and physical processes that we call life. There are about 100 million million cells in the body, of more than 20 main kinds, such as muscle cells and skin cells. Each has a special shape, adapted for the job it does. A group of cells and the substances in which they live make up a tissue.

Ancient beliefs
In ancient times, people had only the vaguest ideas about how the body worked. Traditions and religions often forbade them to cut open, or dissect, the body to study its parts. One of the first great body-scientists was the Roman physician Claudius Galen (AD 129-201). Galen was medical officer for the gladiators who fought bloody battles in the arenas of Ancient Rome. He wrote many books, and his reputation was so great that doctors followed his ideas – even the many wrong ones – for 1,500 years afterwards.

Organs

An organ is a part of the body with a particular job to do. Some organs are located in body cavities. The heart and lungs are found in the chest cavity, which is separated from the abdominal cavity by the diaphragm. The stomach, intestines, liver, kidneys and reproductive organs are located in the abdominal cavity, as shown below. Other organs are found throughout the body, such as bones and muscles.

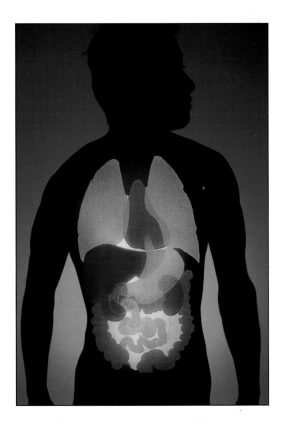

Systems

The organs combine into systems, which are the body's main working units. For example, the lungs and the air passages that lead to them make up the respiratory system (see pages 10-11). The heart, arteries, veins and other blood vessels, and the blood itself, make up the circulatory system (see pages 14-15). The brain and nerves form the nervous system, which controls body processes (pages 24-5). The human body has a dozen of these main working units, explored in this book.

Bodywords

In Ancient Greece and Rome, physicians believed that the parts of the body were made from different mixtures of four fluids, or humours. These were blood (sanguis), phlegm (pituita), black bile (melanchole) and yellow bile (chole). They were connected to the four essences that made up all matter: air, water, fire and earth. These old beliefs gave rise to many words we still use today. A person in a sad mood is said to be melancholic, because these feelings were thought to be caused by an excess of black bile. Words such as phlegmatic, bilious and sanguine have similar origins.

Looking into the body

In the 1600s, the microscope was used with great skill by a Dutch scientist, Anton van Leeuwenhoek. By the late 1600s, great anatomists such as Marcello Malpighi were using the microscope to look into the body and discover cells and other tiny parts. Their work laid the foundations of micro-anatomy. Doctors today use scans of various kinds to look inside the body. Unlike ordinary X-rays, which show only bones, these scans show all the soft parts of the body, such as muscles and nerves. A Magnetic Resonance Image (MRI) can reveal the structure of the brain, spine and facial tissues (below).

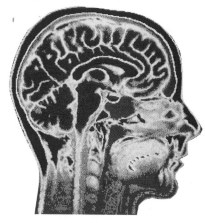

BONES AND JOINTS

The human body is supported by the hard, strong framework of the skeleton. A single bone is stiff and unbending. But the body can bend and move because most of the bones are linked to each other at flexible, moveable joints. Living bones are not dry and brittle, like bones in museums. They are one-third water; the rest is composed of crystals of minerals such as calcium, and a protein called collagen. Bones have a good supply of blood and nerves, and are just as alive and active as the muscles and other soft parts around them.

The skeleton

There are 206 bones in the average human skeleton. A few people have more or less. For example, one person in 20 has an extra pair of ribs, making 13 pairs. Each bone is shaped to protect and support the soft parts around it. The skull, for instance, encloses and protects the brain. There are 32 bones in each arm and hand, and 30 in each leg and foot. The spine or backbone is a column of 26 closely-linked bones called vertebrae. The biggest bones are the femurs, in the thighs. The smallest are the three tiny bones known as the auditory ossicles, in each ear (see page 20). These bones are about the size of rice grains.

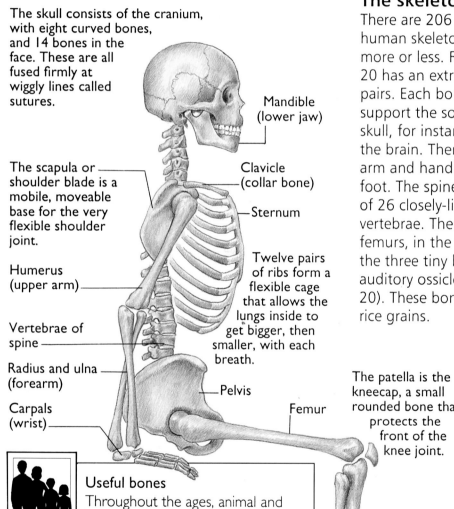

The skull consists of the cranium, with eight curved bones, and 14 bones in the face. These are all fused firmly at wiggly lines called sutures.

Mandible (lower jaw)

The scapula or shoulder blade is a mobile, moveable base for the very flexible shoulder joint.

Clavicle (collar bone)

Sternum

Humerus (upper arm)

Twelve pairs of ribs form a flexible cage that allows the lungs inside to get bigger, then smaller, with each breath.

Vertebrae of spine

Radius and ulna (forearm)

Carpals (wrist)

Pelvis

Femur

The patella is the kneecap, a small rounded bone that protects the front of the knee joint.

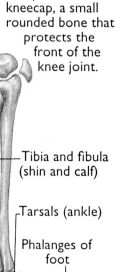

Useful bones
Throughout the ages, animal and human bones have been used as tools, symbols, ornaments and decorations in many societies. Animal bones, along with chipped stones, were probably among the first tools used by prehistoric humans.

Tibia and fibula (shin and calf)

Tarsals (ankle)

Phalanges of foot

False colour X-ray of hand of a two-year old

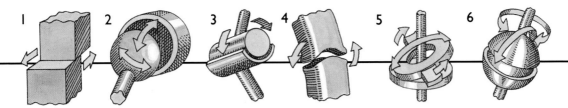

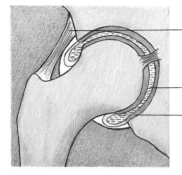

Elastic ligaments hold the bones together.

Joint capsule contains fluid that "oils" the joint.

Smooth cartilage covers the ends of the bones where they touch.

Bones and X-rays

Inside a joint, above, two bones are connected, yet are still able to move. In X-ray photos, bones show up as white shapes. X-rays can detect broken (fractured) bones, or abnormalities as the skeleton grows and matures. Compare the X-ray below, of an adult human hand, with the one on the opposite page. These X-rays illustrate how the bones in the hand and wrist grow and strengthen during childhood.

Types of joints

There are many different kinds of joints in the human body. Among the most important are the plane joint (1) which allows small gliding movements between the vertebrae of the spine, and the ball-and-socket joint (2), found in the hip and shoulder, which allows the limbs to rotate. The hinge joint (3) is found in the knee and elbow, and the saddle joint (4) in the base of the thumb. A pivot joint (5) allows the neck to move freely, and ellipsoid joints (6) connect the lower arm to the wrist, and the lower leg to the ankle.

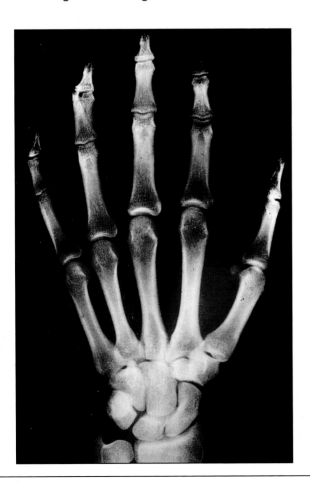

The short and the tall

There are wide variations in the sizes of human bodies, both within one group of people, and between different groups around the world. These variations are based on the sizes of the bones. One of the tallest human groups, the Dinkas, and the smallest, the Pygmies, both come from Africa. Most Pygmies are between 1.2 and 1.4 metres tall. The tendency in developed regions such as Europe and North America is for people from all ethnic groups to become bigger, due to better health care and diet. A bone expert can tell at a glance whether a skeleton comes from a man or a woman, a large child or a small adult.

Two adult Pygmies stand beside a Western man of Caucasian origin.

MUSCLES AND MOVEMENT

All the body's movements are powered by muscles. Muscle tissue is specialised to contract, or get shorter. The body has three main kinds of muscles. One is the skeletal muscles, attached to the bones of the skeleton, which you use to move about. There are more than 600 skeletal muscles, from the huge gluteus in the buttock, to tiny finger and toe muscles. The other kinds of muscles are cardiac muscle in the heart (top left above) and smooth muscles in the stomach, intestines and other internal organs (left above).

Inside a muscle

A skeletal muscle has a bulging central part known as the body. This tapers at each end into a rope-like tendon, which anchors the muscle to a bone. As the muscle contracts, the tendons pull on their bones and move the body. The muscle body is divided into bundles of hair-fine fibres called myofibres. These long cells contain proteins that slide past one another to make the cell shorter in length.

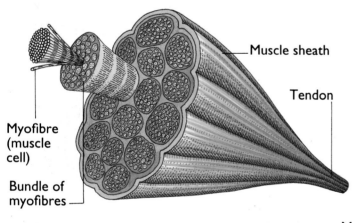

Muscle sheath

Tendon

Myofibre (muscle cell)

Bundle of myofibres

Front shoulder muscle moves shoulder and upper arm.

Neck muscle moves head.

Biceps twists and bends elbow.

Muscles in forearm bend fingers.

Front thigh muscle straightens knee.

Shin muscle bends ankle by pulling up foot.

Changing fashions

Bulging muscles have been in and out of fashion through the centuries. A few hundred years ago, plump bodies were seen as desirable. Today some men and women like to look slim. Other people work hard at body-building, training and lifting weights in the gym. They strive to increase the thickness of their muscle fibres through special exercises and diet.

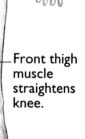

Stories of the strong

Legends from many different cultures tell of well-muscled, strong men and women. Some are heroes, others are villains. Hercules of Ancient Greece had to undertake 12 "herculean" (very difficult) tasks or labours. In the Bible, the boy David fought and killed the giant Goliath with his slingshot. Samson was a hero who fought the Philistines, but he lost his strength when Delilah tricked him into having his hair shorn. Blinded and chained, he pushed the columns of the Gaza Temple and brought it crashing down on himself and his captors, as pictured right.

Triceps contracts, straightening elbow. Biceps relaxes and stretches.

Master of art and science

During the Renaissance period, from about the 14th century, there was a rebirth of fascination in the beauty of the human form, and a scientific interest in the structure and workings of the body. Foremost in this field was the genius of art and science, Leonardo da Vinci (1452-1519). He performed amazing dissections of the body, especially the muscle system, and drew them with unparalled skill and mastery, as shown here.

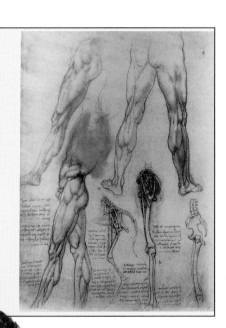

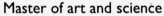

Biceps contracts, bending elbow. Triceps relaxes.

Quadriceps contracts, straightening knee.

Hamstring muscles relax and stretch.

Quadriceps and hamstrings tensed to maintain crouched position.

Muscle pairs

A muscle contracts to pull on its bone. But it cannot do the reverse – actively get longer and push the bone the other way. So many of the body's muscles are arranged in opposing pairs, attached across the same joint. One partner of the pair pulls the bones one way, bending the joint. The other pulls the other way and straightens the joint, while its partner relaxes. Even a simple movement also involves many other muscles that keep the body balanced.

LUNGS AND BREATHING

Nearly all living things, apart from some microbes (tiny organisms), need a supply of oxygen. Oxygen is necessary for the chemical reactions inside a cell known as cellular respiration. These reactions break up nutrients from food, such as sugars, and set free the energy for driving the cell's life processes. The human body gets its oxygen supplies from the air, which is one-fifth oxygen. We breathe air into our lungs, where oxygen is absorbed into the blood and sent around the body. The nose, throat, windpipe, and the two lungs are all involved in breathing; together they are called the respiratory system.

A new chemical element

Oxygen was discovered to be a chemical element, and vital in breathing, by a series of experiments carried out by scientists such as Joseph Priestley (1733-1804), Carl Wilhelm Scheele (1742-86) and Antoine Lavoisier (1743-94, below). Lavoisier named the substance oxygen and discovered it was necessary for burning, and for living things to breathe. This was proved when scientists put animals into glass jars and sucked out the air. This sounds cruel today, since we know that the animals would suffocate and die. But those early experiments helped to explain why life depends on oxygen.

Nasal passage
Breathed-in air flows through the nose, where small hairs filter out bits of dust and floating particles. Sneezing also clears dust particles from the nose.

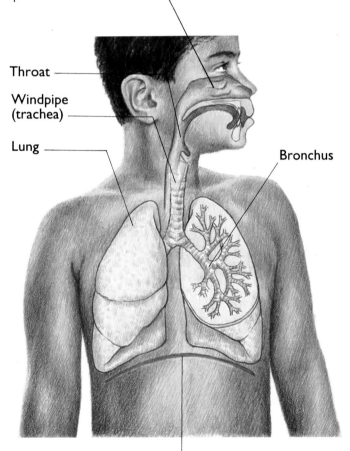

Throat

Windpipe (trachea)

Lung

Bronchus

Windpipe
The windpipe divides into two main airways, the bronchi. Their insides are lined with a sticky fluid, mucus, that traps dirt, and tiny hairs that propel the dirty mucus to the top of the windpipe, where it can be swallowed.

Diaphragm
The chest is filled by the two lungs, the heart and the main blood vessels. The diaphragm is a dome-shaped muscle sheet that forms the base of the chest and the roof of the abdomen. It is the main breathing muscle.

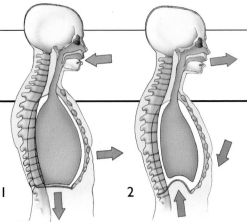

Breathing

Breathing not only obtains vital oxygen. It also gets rid of carbon dioxide. To breathe in, the diaphragm muscle contracts, pulling down the bases of the lungs. The intercostal muscles around the ribs also pull the front of the chest up and out. These movements expand the lungs, sucking in air (1). To breathe out, the diaphragm relaxes. The lungs spring back to their smaller size, puffing out air (2).

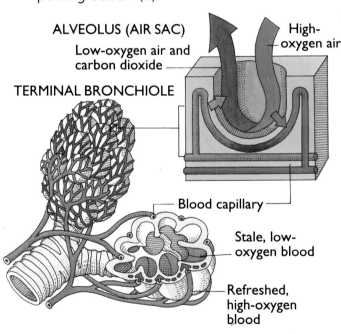

ALVEOLUS (AIR SAC)

Low-oxygen air and carbon dioxide

High-oxygen air

TERMINAL BRONCHIOLE

Blood capillary

Stale, low-oxygen blood

Refreshed, high-oxygen blood

Inside the lung

The main bronchus (airway) of each lung divides more than 15 times. These airways become smaller, until they form thousands of hair-thin air tubes called terminal bronchioles. The bronchioles end at microscopic air sacs known as alveoli. In the alveoli, oxygen seeps from fresh, breathed-in air, through the very thin linings, into the blood flowing through capillaries (tiny blood vessels) on the other side. Blood distributes the oxygen around the body, and carries carbon dioxide back to the lungs, where it is breathed out as stale air.

Recycled breath

Exhaled or breathed-out air contains less oxygen and more carbon dioxide than normal fresh air. But there is still enough oxygen to keep the body going for a couple more breaths. When first-aiders carry out mouth-to-mouth resuscitation (below), they breathe their own air into the patient's lungs. Great escapologist Harry Houdini (1874-1926) is said to have re-breathed his exhaled air a few times, during the daring escapes he staged underwater.

Cooling the fire

For thousands of years, people wondered why we breathe air. The Ancient Greeks such as Plato and Aristotle believed that nutrients from food were burned in the heart to make a "vital flame" that brought warmth and life to the body. They thought that the breathed-in air helped to keep the fire controlled.

Exercise is good for you

Aerobic means "with oxygen". Aerobic exercise makes the body's muscles increase their demands for oxygen, because they are using up more energy, thereby making the lungs and heart work harder. In general, this type of exercise improves the health of the lungs, heart and blood system. In anaerobic ("without oxygen") exercise, the muscles work for short bursts, without immediately increasing their need for oxygen.

DIGESTION

Energy makes things happen. Every living thing, and every machine, needs energy to power its inner processes. The human body's energy comes from its food. Food also supplies the raw materials and building-blocks for bodily growth and repair. The set of organs that gets food into the body, breaks it down or digests it, and absorbs it into the blood, is called the digestive system. It includes the mouth and teeth, gullet, stomach and intestines.

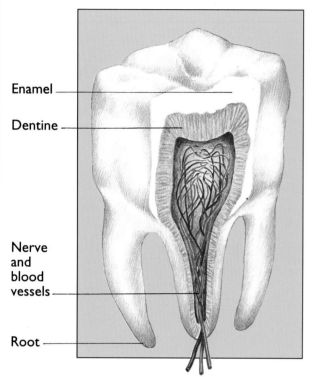

Enamel

Dentine

Nerve and blood vessels

Root

Teeth

Prehistoric people did not have knives and forks. Like wild animals, they used their teeth to cut off and chew mouthfuls of raw food. Today we have cooking and cutlery, but teeth are still important – especially for thorough chewing, which helps the body to digest food more effectively. A tooth is covered with pale enamel, the hardest substance in the body. Under this is dentine, a shock-absorbing barrier. Inside the tooth are a good supply of blood vessels, and the nerves that warn of toothache. Babies grow a first set of milk teeth, 20 in number (in pink above left). From about the age of six years these fall out naturally, and are gradually replaced by 32 adult or permanent teeth. The main types of teeth are shown on the left below.

Grinders
Premolars and molars crush and chew food. An adult has four premolars and six molars in the upper jaw, and the same in the lower jaw, shown here.

Chisels
Incisors at the front of the mouth cut and snip food. An adult has four incisors in the upper jaw and four in the lower jaw.

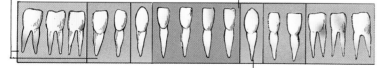

Spears
Canines, next to the incisors, spear and slice food. An adult has two incisors in the upper jaw and two in the lower jaw.

The balanced diet
The science of foods and their effects on the body is called nutrition. There are many differences in foods around the world. Some people eat mainly potatoes, others rice, and others wheat. Yet all these foods contain lots of carbohydrates for energy. A good, healthy diet contains balanced amounts of the substances shown here, plus vitamins and minerals.

Fibre or roughage for digestive-system health
Fruits, leafy vegetables, unrefined breads and cereals and pastas, beans and lentils

Moistening food

Three pairs of salivary glands make watery saliva (spit). This moistens the food for chewing. Digestive chemicals known as enzymes in saliva start to attack the food and break it down.

Pipe through the chest

The gullet is a muscular tube that pushes swallowed food down through the chest, into the stomach. Normally the gullet is squashed flat by the pressure inside the body.

Acid bath

The stomach contains strong digestive enzymes and also hydrochloric acid, made by its lining. This mixture of powerful chemicals further digests the food, for several hours.

Long but narrow

The small intestine contains more enzymes which complete the food's digestion. Nutrients are absorbed through its velvety lining, into the blood that flows through the lining.

The digestive system

This system is like a long tube coiling through the body, about seven metres long. After the mouth and throat, food goes down the gullet into the stomach. Hiccupping may occur if we eat or drink too quickly. The stomach is like a storage bag that expands as it fills with a meal, and squeezes the food into a thick soup. The food passes on to the small intestine, where most nutrients are absorbed. The large intestine takes up much of the water from the left-overs.

Short but wide

The large intestine forms the undigested and left-over contents into semi-soft masses. It stores these until the body is ready to expel them through the ring of muscle at the end of the tube, the anus.

Curious cuisine

Most people in developed regions buy their food from shops. In other regions people hunt and gather food from the wild. Traditional foods vary around the world. Honeypot ants are a delicacy for Australian Aborigines. Mosquito pie is eaten in parts of Africa.

The honeypot ant has sugary fluid in its swollen body. It is a "living larder" for its nest members.

Fats for growth, repair, healthy nerves and energy

Dairy produce, nuts, plants and their products and oils, meat, poultry, fish

Carbohydrates (sugars and starches) for energy

Breads, potatoes, pastas, rice, cereals, fruits

Proteins for body-building

Meat, fish, eggs, cheese, peas, beans and other vegetables

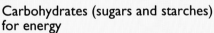

HEART AND CIRCULATION

The body has an efficient transport network to carry supplies and products to where they are needed. It is known as the circulatory system, because its fluid, blood, circulates, or flows round and round, through tubes known as blood vessels. Blood contains three types of cells. Red cells carry oxygen; white cells fight disease (see page 18), and platelets cause blood to clot (see page 19). All these cells float in the liquid part of blood, called plasma. On its endless journey blood distributes nutrients, oxygen and other substances, and collects wastes and by-products.

The blood network

The human body contains between four and five litres of blood, which travels round in an endless one-way circuit. Large, muscular, thick-walled vessels called arteries carry blood from the heart. They branch into smaller tubes, which divide further to become capillaries. A capillary's wall is so thin that oxygen and nutrients can easily seep through to the cells beyond, while carbon dioxide and other wastes seep from the cells into the blood. The capillaries join together to make larger tubes, which come together to form large, thin-walled veins. The main veins take blood back to the heart.

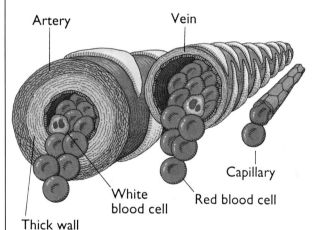

Artery

Vein

Thick wall

White blood cell

Red blood cell

Capillary

Harvey's heart

The English physician William Harvey (1578-1657) realised that the heart was a pump, which forced blood around the body. His discoveries began the modern age of scientific medicine.

The **carotid artery** brings fresh "red" blood from the left side of the heart to the head.

The **jugular vein** returns stale, low-oxygen "blue" blood from the head to the heart.

The **aorta** leads from the left side of the heart, to supply fresh blood to the head, arms, lower body and legs.

The **vena cavae** bring stale blood from the upper and lower body, to the right side of the heart.

The **pulmonary arteries** take stale blood from the right side of the heart to the lungs, for fresh supplies of oxygen.

The **pulmonary veins** take refreshed blood from the lungs to the left side of the heart.

The **femoral artery and vein** take blood to and from each leg.

Blood groups
In the 1900s, Karl Landsteiner (1868-1943) and other scientists discovered blood groups. They showed that blood from certain groups could not mix safely with blood from other groups. Today blood transfusions are commonplace and safe, replacing blood lost through injury or an operation. Blood can only be stored for a few months, so it is important for people to keep giving fresh supplies.

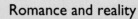

Romance and reality
The heart is a symbol of love and romance. Cards with hearts and romantic messages are exchanged on February 14, the anniversary of St Valentine, an early Christian martyr (below). Literature is full of references to the heart as the seat of love, courage and emotions. But the heart is simply a muscular pump, though an amazingly reliable one. True, it does flutter, miss a beat or speed up during passionate moments. But this is under control from the brain.

The heart has two sides, each with two chambers. The right atrium (upper chamber) receives blood from the main veins.

The left atrium receives blood from the lungs along the pulmonary veins, and pumps it into the left ventricle.

Aorta

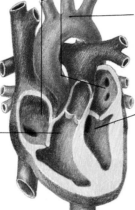

Blood is pumped into the right ventricle. This sends out blood to the lungs to get oxygen.

The muscular heart wall is thickest in the left ventricle. This chamber must pump out blood through the aorta to the whole body.

The pulse
When the body is active, the muscles need more oxygen and nutrients. So the heart pumps faster and harder. With each beat, a bulging pressure wave of blood passes out along the arteries. This is known as the pulse. When you are resting, your pulse rate is about 70-75 beats per minute. After strenuous exercise your pulse rate may more than double.

The heartbeat
When you are at rest, the heart squeezes once a second. Blood oozes into the atria (1), and is pumped through the heart valves into the ventricles (2). The ventricles' muscular walls contract to pump out the blood (3). The cycle starts again (4).

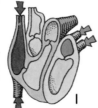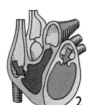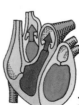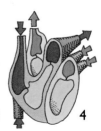

1 2 3 4

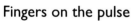

Fingers on the pulse
You can hear a person's heartbeat by placing your ear on his or her chest, slightly to the left. Find the pulse of the radial artery in the inside of the wrist, or of the carotid artery in the neck under the side of the jaw. Feel gently with your fingers, not your thumb, since this has its own small pulse that may cause confusion.

WASTES AND HORMONES

The body's life processes produce dozens of wastes and by-products. These are collected by the endlessly circulating blood, and dealt with mainly by the liver and kidneys, the chief organs of the excretory (waste-disposal) system. In addition, blood circulates special body chemicals called hormones. These control various internal processes such as digestion, fluid balance, growth, and maturing from a child into an adult woman or man.

Processing foods
The liver is the largest organ in the body. It has a rich blood supply from the stomach and intestines, and receives digested nutrients. It makes toxic (poisonous) substances safe, stores some vitamins and carbohydrates, and converts nutrients into useful forms.

Filtering blood
The kidneys are blood-filters. Inside each kidney, one million microscopic filter units called nephrons take waste products such as urea from the blood, along with excess water. These wastes-and-water form the liquid urine, that trickles down the ureters to the bladder.

Ureter

Doing two jobs
The pancreas has two distinct roles. One is to make strong digestive enzymes. These pour along the pancreatic duct into the small intestine, to digest food. The other role is to produce hormones such as insulin.

Testing urine
During the Middle Ages many physicians believed that a patient's urine could show exactly what was wrong with him or her. The urine in a glass tube was held up to the light and examined carefully. This process, called urinoscopy, continued for several centuries until physicians realised it was not very accurate. Today urine is still examined and used to detect diabetes and other diseases, but this is usually done by chemical tests in the laboratory.

Dealing with wastes
The body makes several types of wastes. Digestive left-over wastes are expelled through the anus. Some blood by-products are processed and altered in the liver. The unwanted substance carbon dioxide is breathed out through the lungs. The main wastes in the blood are removed as a fluid called urine, by the urinary system. This system is made up of the two kidneys, the bladder, the ureter tubes which link kidneys and bladder, and the urethra that empties the bladder to the outside.

Urethra

Storing urine
The bladder is a balloon-like storage bag for urine. When it holds about 200-300 millilitres, stretch sensors in its wall send messages along nerves to the brain, signalling that it needs emptying.

Master gland
The pituitary just under the brain makes several hormones and similar chemicals that control other hormonal glands around the body.

Energy regulator
The thyroid gland is shaped like a bow tie in the lower neck. It makes thyroxine, that affects processes such as the way the body uses energy.

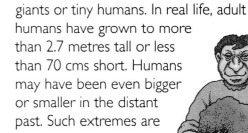

The long and the short of it
Stories about very tall or short people exist in many cultures. Such stories are often exaggerated into legends of giants or tiny humans. In real life, adult humans have grown to more than 2.7 metres tall or less than 70 cms short. Humans may have been even bigger or smaller in the distant past. Such extremes are often due to too much or too little growth hormone, made by the pituitary gland.

Insulin factory
The pancreas produces the hormone insulin, which controls the way cells take in and use energy-containing sugars.

Chemical control
Hormones are the body's chemical messengers. Each is made in a certain gland. The hormone circulates in the blood and affects specific cells and tissues, making them work faster or slower, or releasing their products. Along with the brain and nerves, hormones help the body to function as a coordinated whole.

Female sex glands
In a woman, the ovaries produce the eggs that can grow into babies if fertilised. They produce hormones that help to control the process of maturing from girl to woman, and the monthly menstrual cycle.

Male sex glands
In a man, the testes are small egg-shaped glands hanging below the abdomen in a skin bag, the scrotum. They produce the sperm for reproduction. They also produce hormones that help to control the maturing from boy to man (see page 28).

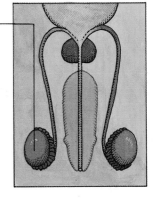

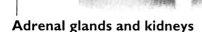

Adrenal glands and kidneys
The adrenal gland on top of each kidney makes a hormone connected with the balance of body water and salts, and adrenalin, that prepares the body for emergency action. The kidneys produce renin, which regulates fluid content and blood pressure.

BODY DEFENCES

The world is full of "germs". They are in the air we breathe, in the soil, on plants and animals, even on our skin, and in some of the food we eat. Some are harmful microbes, such as the bacteria and viruses that cause diseases. The body has several lines of defence against them, including the outer covering of skin, and two systems with scattered parts, the lymphatic and immune systems. In some cases, once the body has defeated a type of germ it is always protected, or immune, against it.

Lymphatic and immune systems

Lymph is the body's "other blood". Lymph fluid collects in the spaces between cells, is channelled into tubes called lymph ducts, and flows through lymph nodes, where it is filtered and cleaned. Travelling round the body, lymph distributes fats and digested nutrients, and collects wastes, which are returned to the blood and filtered out by the kidneys. Lymph, and the blood itself, carry the germ-fighting white blood cells that form the basis of the immune system. These cells recognise germs and make chemicals called antibodies that kill them.

The lymph network

The lymphatic system is body-wide, like the circulatory system. There are collections of bean-sized lymph nodes in the armpits, groin and other places. The lymph ducts finally come together into large tubes that empty into main veins, near the heart.

Lymph node (left)

Lymph fluid flows slowly through the node, where cells are added, broken down and recycled according to the body's needs. In particular, white cells from the blood are stored and multiply, ready to fight germs.

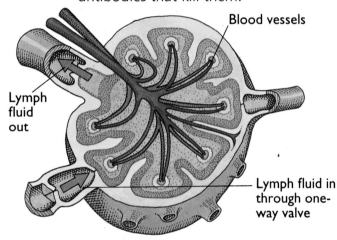

Blood vessels

Lymph fluid out

Lymph fluid in through one-way valve

Vaccination

Blood and lymph contain billions of germ-killing white blood cells. The body can be tricked into defending itself, by injecting it with disabled versions of real germs. These prepare the body so that if real germs invade, they are killed at once. This process, vaccination, was introduced by a British doctor, Edward Jenner (1749-1823, right). In 1796 Jenner successfully vaccinated a patient against the disease smallpox.

Deadly rhyme

"Ring-a-ring-a-roses, A pocket full of posies, A-tishoo, A-tishoo, We all fall down." This nursery rhyme originated at the time of the Great Plague, which swept Britain in 1665. As the plague spread, people carried posies of flowers, hoping the scent would prevent the disease. If they fell ill, one of the first signs was sneezing, and death would follow. Plague pits were dug (right) to dispose of the bodies and to try to prevent further spread of the disease.

Splinter

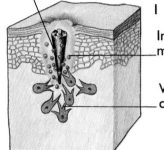

1

Infecting microbes

White cells

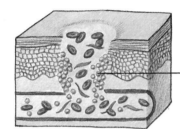

2

Blood plasma and platelets begin to form clot.

3

Wound is sealed

Sealing wounds

Small cuts and wounds happen all the time, inside the body and outside on the skin. At a wound, no matter how small, blood undergoes a chain of chemical changes. If the skin is punctured, for example by a splinter (above), the blood becomes thicker and sticky, and white cells gather to attack any germs that may try to get in (1). As the splinter is removed, tiny cell fragments that normally float in the blood, known as platelets, become stuck in the stickiness and make a gooey barrier. This process is known as coagulating or clotting (2). The clot goes hard and seals the wound, to stop blood and body fluids leaking out, and to prevent dirt and germs getting in (3). Gradually the skin or other tissue grows back and heals itself.

Healers through the ages

Different societies have many types of healers or shamans. In prehistory, shamans may have worn the skins of animals during ceremonies (left). Modern medicine relies on factory-produced drugs, chemical tests, advanced surgery and complicated equipment. There is no doubt that it has been amazingly successful. But there has been renewed interest in traditional medicines that use natural products, and place more importance on the mind and soul.

AIDS

One of today's greatest health challenges is AIDS, Acquired Immune Deficiency Syndrome. A microbe called HIV (Human Immunodeficiency Virus) infects the body and attacks the immune system, so the body cannot protect itself against other microbes. Millions of people around the world have HIV. Drugs slow the course of this fatal disease, but no cure has been discovered yet.

A human cell infected with HIV

SIGHT AND HEARING

An animal needs to sense the world around it, in order to find food and drink, locate shelter and mates, and detect and move away from danger. The organs specialised to do this form the sensory system. They are closely connected to the nervous system. The human body's five main senses are sight, hearing, smell, taste and touch. Our sense of balance is also vital. This involves the semicircular canals in the ears, and information from the skin about touch, from stretch detectors in the muscles in joints about body position and from the eyes about head position.

Inside the ear

The ear detects patterns of sound waves travelling through the air. The outer ear flap funnels sound waves into a 25-millimetre-long tube, the outer ear canal. At the end of this tube is the eardrum, which vibrates as sound waves bounce off it. The vibrations pass along a chain of three tiny bones, the ear ossicles, and into the fluid inside the cochlea. There the vibrations are transformed into electrical signals known as nerve impulses, which flash along nerves to the brain.

Eustachian tube

The Eustachian tube leads between your ear and throat. It opens during swallowing and yawning, to equalise air pressure within the ear.

Outer ear flap

Sense of balance

The semi-circular canals are involved in balance. They are filled with fluid. As the head tilts, tiny hair cells in the fluid move, sending signals to the brain.

Hammer (malleus)
Anvil (incus)
Stirrup (stapes)

Outer ear canal

The cochlea

A delicate membrane inside the cochlea is covered with microscopic cells that have hairs sticking from them. The vibrating fluid in the cochlea shakes the hairs and generates nerve impulses from the cells.

Eustachian tube to throat

The eardrum

This disc of tightly-stretched, skin-type tissue is about as big as the nail on the little finger. Like skin, it can heal itself if slightly cut or torn.

Hard of hearing

People who are deaf (unable to hear) have been at a great disadvantage in the past. Ear trumpets, that collect sound waves and concentrate them into the ear, have been used for centuries. A Victorian version is shown here. Today deaf people learn lip-reading, and sign language with the hands. Modern electronic hearing aids can also help some deaf people.

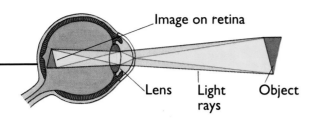

Image on retina

Lens / Light rays / Object

Inside the eye

The eye is a sphere about 25 millimetres across, filled with clear jelly. It is specialised to detect patterns of light rays and transform them into tiny electrical signals, nerve impulses, which flash along nerves to the brain. At the front of the eye is a clear domed part, the cornea. Behind this is a coloured ring, the iris, with a hole in the centre, the pupil. Behind the pupil is a clear bulging disc, the lens, which bends the light rays. Light rays pass through the cornea, pupil and lens, into the interior of the eye. They shine on a very thin layer lining the inside, the retina. This contains more than 120 million cells known as rods and cones, because of their shape. The rods and cones turn the colours, patterns and brightnesses of light-ray energy into nerve-signal energy, and send the nerve impulses along the optic nerve to the brain for analysis.

The world upside down?

Because of the way a lens works, the image it shines onto the retina is upside down. But a baby's brain has no concept of up or down. It learns to turn the images "right side up" almost from the very beginning, as a natural part of sight.

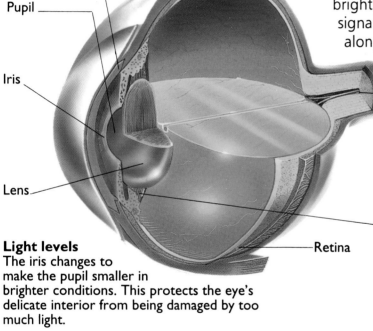

Cornea

Pupil

Iris

Lens

Optic nerve

Retina

Light levels
The iris changes to make the pupil smaller in brighter conditions. This protects the eye's delicate interior from being damaged by too much light.

Focusing
A ring of muscles makes the lens bulge fatter for near objects, and stretch thinner for faraway ones, to focus light rays clearly on the retina.

Better sight
Spectacles and contact lenses change the path of light rays, so that people whose eyes cannot focus properly are able to see clearly and sharply. The first spectacles were in use by the 13th century. The system of Braille allows blind people to read, by running their fingers over tiny patterns of raised dots on the page. It was invented in 1824 by Louis Braille (1809-1852), a blind French student, when he was 15.

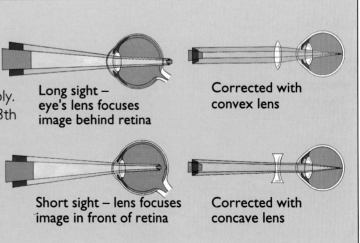

Long sight – eye's lens focuses image behind retina

Corrected with convex lens

Short sight – lens focuses image in front of retina

Corrected with concave lens

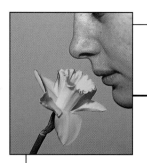

SMELL, TASTE, TOUCH

The human body's main senses are sight and hearing. However, our sense of smell is also important, helping us to identify things at a distance, unlike taste and touch. Taste is similar to smell, but detects flavour substances in foods and drinks, rather than odour substances floating through the air. Both these senses check that foods and drinks are not bad or rotten, as revealed by unpleasant odours and flavours. The skin also has a warning function, signalling if the body is in danger from extreme heat, cold or pressure.

Inside the nose and mouth

Air carrying odour substances passes through the nasal cavity as you breathe in and out. The odours land on a batch of toothbrush-like olfactory hairs, in the roof of the cavity. Microscopic cells attached to the hairs send nerve impulses to the brain when they detect certain odours. Similarly, flavour substances from foods are detected by tiny, onion-shaped groups of cells known as taste buds. These are scattered over the tongue, among the larger lumps and bumps known as papillae. The taste bud cells send nerve impulses to the brain when they recognise four main flavours: sweet, salty, sour and bitter.

Olfactory hairs

Olfactory nerve to brain

Nasal cavity

Papillae

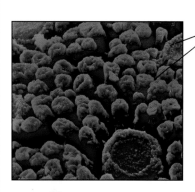

Tongue

Tongue muscle

Testing smell and taste
Test your senses of smell and taste by trying this experiment with a friend. Prepare small samples of sweet, sour, salt and bitter foods. See if you can tell which sample is which when you are blindfolded. Then try the experiment again, holding your nose. How successful are you this time at detecting different tastes?

Taste buds

An average person has about 10,000 taste buds. They are located mainly on the tongue, among the tiny projections known as fungi-form papillae that appear in pink in the magnified false-colour image on the left above. Conical papillae (blue) form a rough surface that helps in the chewing of food. There are also taste buds on the insides of the cheeks, on the roof of the mouth, and on the upper throat.

Sweaty lies

When people are nervous, they tend to sweat. This reduces the skin's resistance to small, harmless amounts of electricity. The polygraph or "lie detector" measures the electrical resistance of the skin. It has been used to test whether people are calm and probably innocent when questioned, or nervous and perhaps guilty.

Skin colour

Groups of people who have traditionally lived in certain parts of the world have different skin colours. Where the Sun's rays are strong, skin makes more of its natural dark colouring substance, melanin. This protects the tissues beneath from the Sun's potentially harmful UV (ultra-violet) rays. Over thousands of years, evolution has produced dark skin, compared to the light-coloured skin of people who live in temperate regions.

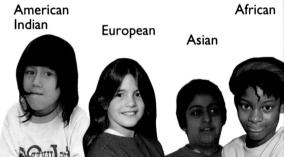

American Indian   European   Asian   African

Epidermis
This is the fast-multiplying layer that forms the surface coating of dead cells.

Sebaceous gland oils the skin

Hair root

Sweat pore

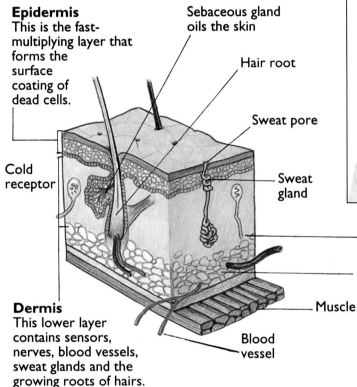

Cold receptor

Sweat gland

Light touch receptor (Meissner's corpuscle)

Fat layer

Dermis
This lower layer contains sensors, nerves, blood vessels, sweat glands and the growing roots of hairs.

Muscle

Blood vessel

Sensors

In addition to the cold and light touch receptors shown, the skin contains sensors for heat, pain and pressure.

The skin

The skin is the body's supple, protective coat. It helps to keep out too much heat, cold, water, germs and harmful rays, and keep in body warmth and fluids. Its surface consists of microscopic skin cells, dead and hardened with the substance keratin. Every day, millions of these cells are worn away as the body moves, wears clothes, and washes. They are replaced by cells below multiplying and moving upwards. Under this layer are microscopic sensors that detect touch, pressure, pain, heat and cold. Under the dermis is a layer of fat, which absorbs shocks, and helps insulate the body from heat and cold.

Washing is fashionable

Thorough personal hygiene, with daily washes, is relatively recent. In the past, the nearest running water was the local river. Rich people used perfumes to mask their body odours. By the last century, people knew that some germs cause disease. They began to wash more often, sometimes helped by a maid (right).

NERVES AND REACTIONS

Along with hormones (see pages 16-17), nerves control and coordinate the whole body, and make it respond to information about the outside world obtained by the senses. The nervous system has two main parts. One is the central system, consisting of the brain and spinal cord. The other is the peripheral system. This includes the thin interconnected nerves snaking all through the body, which link the central system to the organs and tissues. There are more than 50,000 kilometres of nerves in the body.

Automatic nerves

The nerve network shown here deals mainly with information for the conscious brain – things you are aware of, and can control. Running alongside it is another nerve network, mainly in the chest and abdomen. This is the autonomic network. It deals with vital processes such as heartbeat, regular breathing, digestion, waste disposal and blood pressure. It is controlled by the brain, but works automatically, in the subconscious.

Body artist

During the Renaissance period, Andreas Vesalius (1514-64) followed Leonardo da Vinci as a great artistic anatomist. Born in Brussels, he became medical professor at Padua in Italy at the age of 23, where he dissected and studied human bodies, and drew beautifully accurate pictures of what he saw. He corrected the traditional teachings of Galen (see page 4), which offended many people. Vesalius' book *De Humanis Corporis Fabrica* (*On the Structure of the Human Body*), in 1543, began the era of scientific anatomy.

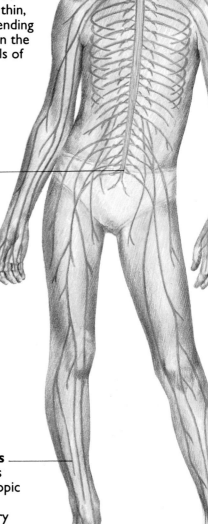

Brain
The brain is the control centre for the whole body (see pages 26-27). Like the rest of the nervous system, it is made of interconnected nerve cells. Each one has thin, wire-like parts extending from it, that pass on the tiny electrical signals of nerve impulses.

Spinal cord
This thick bundle of nerves merges into the lower brain. It is sited inside a tunnel in the vertebral bones, where it is protected from knocks. Spinal nerve roots branch out to the various organs and parts.

Peripheral nerves
Each nerve contains bundles of microscopic nerve-cell "wires". Sensory nerves carry signals from sense organs to the brain. Motor nerves take signals from the brain to the muscles.

Madness and bedlam

Brain disorders are some of the most unsettling of all illnesses. In epilepsy, the brain is overcome by random nerve impulses firing through the nerve-cell network. These make the body jerk or convulse, in a fit or seizure. In past times, people with certain brain disorders were labelled as "mad" and locked away in asylums such as Bethlehem, or Bedlam (right). Now drugs and other medical treatments can help many problems.

Fast reactions

Quick reactions help the body to play fast-moving sports, and also to survive and minimise injuries. If a finger touches a flame, the skin's pain sensors send nerve impulses along sensory nerves to the spinal cord, which relays them to the brain. In case the brain does not react in time, the cord also sends impulses straight back along motor nerves, telling the arm muscles to jerk the finger away. This is known as a reflex.

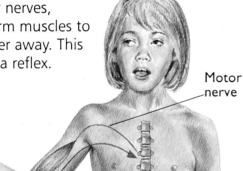

Motor nerve

Pain sensors in skin

Sensory nerve

Skilful coordination

The Ancient Greeks had a great tradition of strength and skill in sports such as running, jumping, spear-hurling, discus-throwing (below), boxing and wrestling. They needed fast reactions and good coordination – activities involving not only the muscles, but the nervous system that controls them. The Greeks held their original Olympic Games every four years from as long ago as 1000 BC. Gradually the games were enlarged to include more running events, and even theatre and music performances. The games were supposed to celebrate the ancient Greek gods, but the winners came to be treated as gods themselves. In AD 394 the games ended. The modern Olympics began in 1896 and carry on the tradition.

Statue in the Olympic Stadium, Athens, Greece

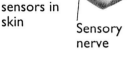

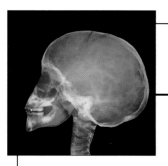

CONTROL CENTRE

The brain is the control centre of the body, and the place where consciousness and the mind are based. Some 100 billion nerve cells, each one connected to up to half a million others, make up an unimaginably complicated network for nerve impulses. Much of the brain's activity does not take place consciously. The "automatic brain" controls heartbeat, breathing, digestion, temperature and many other body processes, without your conscious involvement. Certain areas of the brain are concerned with specific functions.

Thalamus
This egg-shaped part is a relay station between the cortex and the rest of the brain. It filters out or redirects many nerve impulses, so that the "thinking" cortex can concentrate on what is important.

Hypothalamus
Small as a fingertip, the hypothalamus regulates basic urges and desires such as hunger, thirst, heartbeat, breathing, blood pressure, body temperature and sexual activity.

Cortex
This wrinkled sheet of "grey matter", 2-4 millimetres thick, is the outer wrapping for the two cerebral hemispheres that make up nine-tenths of the brain. The cortex deals with thoughts, memories, learning, sensations and body control (see opposite).

Cerebellum
The wrinkled lobes of the cerebellum look like a mini-version of the cerebral hemispheres. They coordinate and organise muscle actions.

Medulla
The lowest part of the brain narrows and merges with the spinal cord. It is involved in automatic processes such as pulse rate, digestion, breathing and chewing.

Reading head bumps

In the 19th century, phrenology was a popular and important "science". A phrenologist was an expert at reading the lumps and bumps on the human skull, which were supposed to reveal the person's intelligence, friendliness, reliability, truthfulness and emotional behaviour, and other aspects of the personality. Phrenology is now seen as fake by modern scientists.

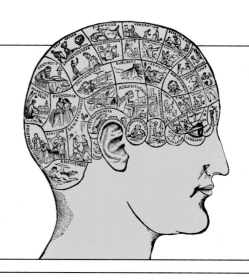

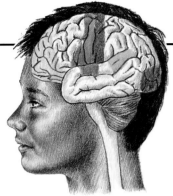

Brain areas
Different areas of the brain's outer cortex are the centres of various kinds of mental activity.

- Reading and understanding
- Hearing
- Speech
- Body motor centre
- Awareness
- Visual
- Body sensory centre

"You are getting sleepy ..."
One mysterious but scientifically recognised feature of the mind-and-brain is hypnosis. This is also called mesmerism after one of its pioneers, Austrian physician Franz Mesmer (1734-1815). The hypnotised person will do many things asked of him or her, and can be "put to sleep". Hypnotism has become a useful technique in treating various mental disorders, easing pain, and controlling obsessions and habits such as gambling and smoking.

Animal brains
Humans are the most intelligent animals on Earth. This is due partly to our large brains, and especially the area of the cortex. More accurately, it is linked to the size of the brain and its cortex, in proportion to the whole body. In general, animals that we consider to be "intelligent" have large brains in relation to their body sizes. The average human brain weighs 1.2-1.4 kilos.

In various mammals, different proportions of the cerebrum are taken up with hearing, seeing and so on, depending on how important those functions are to the animal. Smell is a very important sense for rats and ground shrews, but is less important to chimpanzees. Chimpanzees and other intelligent primates have a much larger proportion of non-specific brain.

Rat   Chimpanzee   Ground shrew

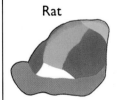 

 Motor   Hearing   Seeing

Smell   Sensory   Non-specific

Head-hunters
Until recent times, some groups of people used to sever and preserve the heads of their enemies, to commemorate victory in battle. Some have even eaten their enemies' brains in an attempt to gain extra courage and wisdom. These traditions were carried out in parts of South America, Papua New Guinea and Indonesia, shown in the illustration on the right. They are now exceptionally rare.

REPRODUCTION

The reproductive systems of women and men are the parts specialised for producing babies. Mating (sexual intercourse) and pregnancy are a natural part of the life cycle, found in all animals. Parents have young, who grow up and have young of their own, and so on. The biological basics of human reproduction are much the same as in our mammal relatives, such as monkeys.

MALE REPRODUCTIVE ORGANS

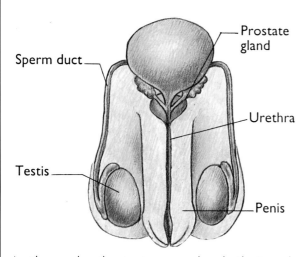

In the male, the testes are glands that make millions of sperm cells. During sex, the man's penis becomes longer and stiffer, and is inserted into the woman's vagina. Sperm come along the urethra and out into the vagina. They swim through the womb and into the egg ducts, towards a ripe egg.

FEMALE REPRODUCTIVE ORGANS

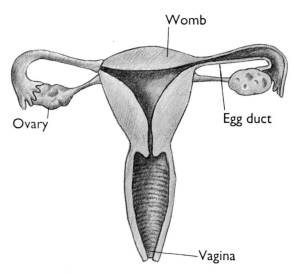

Every four weeks, one of the woman's ovaries releases a tiny ripe egg cell which travels down the egg duct towards the womb. The womb is ready to nourish the fertilised egg. If there is no fertilised egg, the womb lining breaks down and flows out of the vagina as the monthly blood loss or period.

Families big and small

In times gone by, and in some countries today, parents have lots of children. As soon as they are able, the children must work to bring back money for the family. In other parts of the world, parents have only one or two children, and may practise birth control (contraception) to prevent the possibility of having any more. This may be due to personal preference, or lack of money and jobs, or because of their countries' official encouragement for small families.

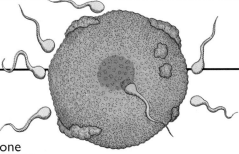

Only one sperm cell fuses with the egg cell to fertilise it.

Fertilisation

An egg cell cannot develop into a baby unless it is fertilised by a sperm cell from the male. The head of one sperm merges into the egg cell (above), and their genetic materials or DNAs come together. The DNAs contain all the instructions, in the form of a chemical code, to make a new living, breathing human body.

The egg cell begins to divide 24 hours after fertilisation.

The secret of life

In 1953, American biologist James Watson (1928-) and English biochemist Francis Crick (1916-) worked out the structure of DNA. Its shape is a double helix, like two intertwined spiral staircases. The strands can separate and copy themselves, as cells divide. The sets of DNA are in the nucleus of the cell, tightly coiled into X-shaped structures called chromosomes. Watson and Crick's discovery explained how general features are passed on from parents to children (right), yet each child (apart from identical twins) is always slightly different.

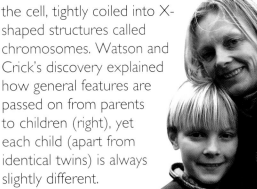

Embryo at six weeks

Foetus at four months, with the umbilical cord that connects it to the mother's placenta

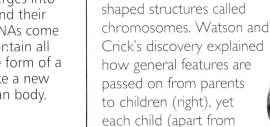

Pregnancy

After fertilisation the egg cell divides, forming a pinhead-sized ball of a hundred or more cells. This settles into the nourishing, blood-rich lining of the womb, and its cells continue to multiply. Gradually the cells become specialised into nerve cells, muscle cells, blood cells and so on, and a tiny baby takes shape. This stage is called the embryo. Two months after fertilisation, the baby is about 25-30 millimetres long. From now until birth, at nine months after fertilisation, it is known as a foetus. At birth the baby passes through the neck of the womb, through the vagina, to the outside world.

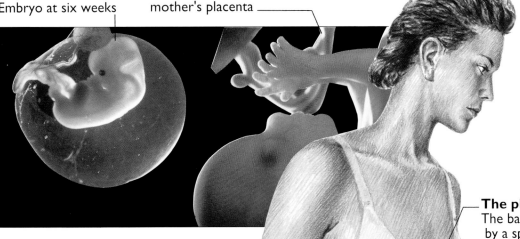

The placenta

The baby is nourished by a special organ called the placenta. This passes nutrients and oxygen from the mother's blood across a thin membrane to the baby's blood, which flows along a "lifeline" called the umbilical cord.

Foetus

Womb

Closed neck of womb

BODYFILE

There are more than 6 billion human bodies on Earth. Millions more have lived and died in the past. During its lifetime, an average body goes through the stages shown below. A new baby is almost helpless. It cannot make its own food, keep itself warm and clean, or move about.

The toddler learns to walk, then talk, and handle items with skill. Next come reading and writing, when the young child may be learning 10-20 new words and their meanings every day, often without realising. Older children learn many complex and abstract subjects at school.

During the teenage years, body changes take place that transform a child into a young adult. A girl develops breasts and rounded hips. Her ovaries begin to produce ripe eggs, and her womb undergoes the monthly changes of the menstrual cycle. A boy becomes more muscular, and his voice deepens. Hair grows on his face and parts of his body, and his testes begin to make sperm. Both boy and girl experience a growth spurt.

During young adulthood, most people are at their peak of physical fitness. As middle age approaches the body becomes less fit, though still as active as the owner wishes. By old age the muscles are less powerful, the reactions are slower, and the skeleton has become slightly smaller. But there are gains of increasing experience and wisdom.

Average lifespan in developed countries: 70-77 years

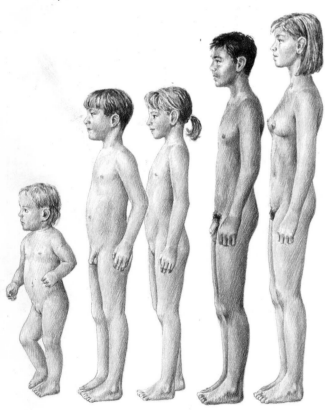
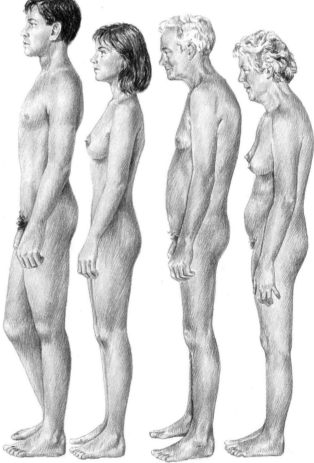

Toddler   Children   Young teenagers   Adults   Older people

The time of fastest growth is in the womb and just after birth. Thereafter, growth gradually slows until the spurt of puberty, which happens from about 10-11 years in most girls, and 12-13 years in most boys. The body reaches its maximum height at about 20 years of age.

The body is up to one centimetre shorter in the evening compared to the morning. Standing and walking during the day slightly compresses the joints between the spinal bones.

GLOSSARY

Anatomy The study of the structure of living things, as opposed to physiology, which is the way they work. Human anatomy is the study of the structure of the human body.

Artery A large tube or vessel that carries blood away from the heart, to the organs and tissues. Most arteries contain bright red, high-oxygen blood. The pulmonary arteries to the lungs contain dark, low-oxygen blood.

Capillaries A network of very small tubes or vessels, finer than hairs. The blood inside them can pass its oxygen and nutrients to the surrounding tissues.

Cartilage A smooth, rubbery or gristly substance. It covers the ends of bones in joints, and forms a flexible framework for parts such as the nose, ears and voice box.

Cell The basic building block of living things. There are billions of cells in the human body, of many different kinds – muscle cells, bone cells, blood cells and so on. An average cell is one-hundredth of a millimetre across and can only be seen with a microscope.

DNA A molecule that contains all the genetic information, which is passed from parents to offspring and tells the body how to develop. DNA is a very long molecule, consisting of two twisted strands.

Enzyme A body substance that speeds up a chemical reaction. The body has hundreds of enzymes. Digestive enzymes speed up the process of digestion, cutting food into smaller pieces.

Gland A body part that makes a substance, usually a liquid, that has a specific use. The pancreas gland makes digestive juices to attack food. Endocrine glands, such as the adrenals, make hormones. In a woman, mammary glands produce milk, which is all the food a new baby needs for the first months of its life.

Hormone A body substance that acts as a "chemical messenger". Made in an endocrine gland, it circulates in the blood, and affects the way certain cells and organs work.

Ligament A strong, slightly stretchy, strap-like part around a joint. Several ligaments hold the bones of a joint together, strengthening and stabilising the joint.

Membrane The thin covering or "skin" over a body cell or larger part.

Muscle A body part specialised to contract, or get shorter. Muscles make all the movements in the body, both inside the body (stomach and guts), and movements of the whole body.

Nerve A body part specialised to carry messages, in the form of tiny electrical signals or pulses. Nerves control and coordinate most body processes.

Organ A major body part that has a distinct function, such as the heart, lung or brain.

Tendon A strong, rope-like part at each end of a muscle. The tendon connects the muscle itself to the bone that it pulls.

Tissue A group of similar cells that all do the same job, such as muscle tissue or nerve tissue. Collections of different tissues make up the major body parts, known as organs.

Vein A large tube or vessel that carries blood back to the heart, from the organs and tissues. Most veins contain dark, low-oxygen blood. The pulmonary veins from the lungs contain bright red, high-oxygen blood.

INDEX

Photocredits
ABBREVIATIONS: T-top, M-middle, B-bottom, L-left, R-right
Cover T & 10 T: Robert Harding Picture Library; cover B & 3T, 12, 13, 14T, 15B, 16, 20T, 22T, 23T, 25BL, 28T & 29T: Roger Vlitos; 2T, 7R, 8 & 24T: Frank Spooner Pictures; 2B, 3M, 9T, 20B, 23B, 25T, 26T & 27 both: Mary Evans Picture Library; 3B, 9B, 10B, 14B, 15T, 18, 19T & 24B: Hulton Deutsch; 4, 5 both, 6, 17, 19B, 22B & 29 ML & MR: Science Photo Library; 11, 25BR, 26T & 28B: Spectrum Colour Library